Revealed: The Truth About Relationships

Gracie Wells

Published by Gracie Wells, 2024.

REVEALED: THE TRUTH ABOUT RELATIONSHIPS

First edition. August 6, 2024.

Copyright © 2024 Gracie Wells.

ISBN: 979-8227974600

Written by Gracie Wells.

To my beautiful mother, the strongest and fearless critic of them all and to all my readers, whose enthusiasm and feedback fuel my creativity and drive.

Introduction

In today's fast-paced digital world, finding and maintaining genuine connections can be daunting. Whether you're diving into online dating, seeking lasting romance, planning a wedding, or looking for relationship-enhancing activities like fun romantic and healthy recipes, this book is your comprehensive guide to modern love. We will also delve into recognizing and healing from toxic relationships, including those involving narcissism.

I'm Gracie Wells, and my journey through the highs and lows of love has equipped me with invaluable insights. From the excitement of online dating to the complexities of recognizing narcissistic behavior, and from planning a marriage to creating lasting romance, I've experienced it all. This book blends my personal experiences with practical advice to support you in building and sustaining meaningful relationships. Together, we'll explore the multifaceted world of love, ensuring you find happiness and fulfillment at every stage.

Chapter 1
Understanding Yourself in the Dating Scene

Knowing Your Values and Priorities. Knowing your values and priorities is crucial when navigating the dating scene as an adult. It is important to take the time to reflect on what is truly important to you in a relationship and what you are looking for in a partner. By understanding your values and priorities, you can make more informed decisions when it comes to dating and relationships.

One of the first steps in knowing your values and priorities is to take the time to reflect on your past relationships and what you have learned from them. Think about what worked well in those relationships and what didn't. Consider the qualities that you value in a partner and what you are looking for in a long-term relationship. By reflecting on your past experiences, you can gain valuable insights into what is truly important to you in a relationship.

Another important aspect of knowing your values and priorities is setting boundaries. It is essential to establish clear boundaries in a relationship and communicate them to your partner. This includes boundaries around communication, personal space, and what you are comfortable with in a relationship. By setting boundaries, you can ensure that your values and priorities are respected and upheld in a relationship.

In addition to setting boundaries, it is important to prioritize self-care and self-love in a relationship. This means taking care of your own emotional and physical well-being and not relying on your partner to fulfill all of your needs. By prioritizing self-care, you can ensure that you are in a healthy and balanced relationship that is based on mutual respect and support.

Ultimately, knowing your values and priorities is essential for finding a fulfilling and meaningful relationship as an adult. By taking the time to reflect on what is important to you, setting boundaries, and prioritizing self-care, you can navigate the dating scene with confidence and clarity. Remember, knowing yourself is the first step to finding a partner who aligns with your values and priorities.

Recognizing Your Emotional Needs. Understanding and acknowledging your emotional needs is a crucial aspect of navigating the dating scene as an adult. Before embarking on a new relationship, it is important to take the time to reflect on what your emotional needs are and how they can be fulfilled in a healthy and fulfilling way. This self-awareness will not only help you communicate your needs to your partner, but also empower you to make decisions that are in alignment with your emotional well-being.

One key aspect of recognizing your emotional needs is identifying what makes you feel loved, supported, and valued in a relationship. This can vary greatly from person to person, so it is important to take the time to reflect on past relationships and experiences to pinpoint what truly matters to you. Whether it's quality time, acts of service, words of affirmation, physical touch, or gifts, understanding your love language can help you communicate your needs effectively to your partner.

It is also important to recognize when your emotional needs are not being met in a relationship. This can manifest in feelings of loneliness, resentment, or dissatisfaction. By tuning into your emotions and paying attention to how you feel in your relationship, you can identify areas where your needs are not being fulfilled and address them with your partner. Remember, it is not selfish to prioritize your emotional well-being in a relationship.

In addition to recognizing your own emotional needs, it is also important to be attuned to the emotional needs of your partner. Communication is key in any relationship, and being able to listen and empathize with your partner's needs can strengthen your bond and create a more fulfilling partnership. By creating a safe space for open and honest communication, you can work together to ensure that both of your emotional needs are being met in the relationship.

Ultimately, recognizing and prioritizing your emotional needs is essential for building healthy and fulfilling relationships as an adult. By taking the time to reflect on what truly matters to you, communicating effectively with your partner, and creating a supportive and understanding environment, you can navigate the dating scene with confidence and authenticity. Remember, your emotional well-being is valuable and deserves to be nurtured in all aspects of your life, including your relationships.

Understanding Your Communication Style. In the world of dating, understanding your communication style is essential for building strong and healthy relationships. Your communication style is the way you express yourself, both verbally and non-verbally, and it plays a significant role in how you interact with others. By recognizing and understanding your communication style, you can improve your relationships and avoid misunderstandings with potential partners.

One common communication style is assertive communication, which involves expressing your thoughts and feelings in a clear and direct manner while also respecting the thoughts and feelings of others. This style is often seen as the most effective for healthy relationships, as it promotes open and honest communication. By being assertive, you can communicate your needs and boundaries effectively, leading to more meaningful connections with others.

On the other hand, passive communication involves avoiding conflict and confrontation, often at the expense of your own needs. This communication style can lead to misunderstandings and resentment in relationships, as your true feelings and desires may not be expressed. It's important to recognize if you tend towards passive communication and work on being more assertive in order to build stronger and more fulfilling relationships.

Another common communication style is aggressive communication, which involves expressing your thoughts and feelings in a forceful and often disrespectful manner. This style can be damaging to relationships, as it can lead to conflict and hurt feelings. If you tend towards aggressive communication, it's important to work on developing more assertive communication skills in order to foster healthier relationships with others.

Finally, passive-aggressive communication involves expressing your feelings indirectly, often through sarcasm, backhanded compliments, or other subtle forms of communication. This style can be damaging to relationships, as it can lead to confusion and misunderstandings. By recognizing if you tend towards passive-aggressive communication and working on being more assertive and direct in your communication, you can improve your relationships and avoid unnecessary conflict. Understanding your communication style is key to navigating the dating scene and building strong, healthy relationships with others. By recognizing your own tendencies and working on developing more assertive communication skills, you can improve your interactions with potential partners and create more meaningful connections in your dating life.

Chapter 2
Preparing for Dating Success

Setting Realistic Expectations. Setting realistic expectations is crucial when navigating the dating scene as an adult. It's easy to get caught up in the excitement of meeting someone new and imagining a perfect future together. However, it's important to remember that relationships take time to develop and grow. By setting realistic expectations, you can avoid disappointment and set yourself up for success in your dating endeavors.

One key aspect of setting realistic expectations is understanding that not every date will lead to a long-term relationship. It's important to approach each date with an open mind and a willingness to get to know the other person without placing too much pressure on the outcome. By keeping an open mind, you can enjoy the experience of meeting new people and potentially forming meaningful connections.

Another important aspect of setting realistic expectations is being honest with yourself about what you are looking for in a relationship. It's essential to know your own values, goals, and boundaries before entering into a new relationship. By being clear about what you want and need from a partner, you can avoid getting into relationships that are not fulfilling or healthy for you.

Setting realistic expectations also means being aware of the fact that not every relationship will be perfect. It's normal to have disagreements and conflicts in any relationship, but it's important to communicate openly and honestly with your partner to resolve issues and move forward together. By setting realistic expectations for the ups and downs of relationships, you can build a strong foundation for a healthy and successful partnership.

In conclusion, setting realistic expectations is essential when navigating the dating scene as an adult. By approaching each date with an open mind, being honest about your own needs and boundaries, and being prepared for the challenges of relationships, you can increase your chances of finding a fulfilling and healthy partnership. Remember that relationships take time to develop, and by setting realistic expectations, you can create a solid foundation for a successful and meaningful relationship.

Building Confidence and Self-Esteem. Building confidence and self-esteem is crucial when navigating the dating scene as an adult. It is important to remember that confidence is not about being perfect or never making mistakes, but rather about accepting yourself as you are and believing in your worth. When you have confidence in yourself, you are more likely to attract others who see your value and treat you with respect.

One way to build confidence and self-esteem is to practice self-care and self-love. Take time to do things that make you feel good about yourself, whether it's getting a massage, going for a walk in nature, or simply taking a few moments to meditate and center yourself. When you prioritize your own well-being, you send a message to yourself and others that you are worthy of love and care.

Another important aspect of building confidence and self-esteem is to challenge negative self-talk and replace it with positive affirmations. It can be easy to fall into the trap of criticizing yourself or doubting your worth, but this only serves to hold you back from reaching your full potential. Instead, try to focus on your strengths and accomplishments, and remind yourself of all the reasons why you are deserving of love and happiness.

Surrounding yourself with supportive and positive people can also help boost your confidence and self-esteem. Seek out friends and family members who lift you up and encourage you to be your best self. Avoid toxic relationships or situations that make you feel small or unworthy, as these can chip away at your confidence and self-esteem over time.

In conclusion, building confidence and self-esteem is an ongoing process that requires self-awareness, self-care, and positive self-talk. By taking the time to invest in yourself and your well-being, you will not only feel better about yourself, but you will also attract healthier and more fulfilling relationships in the dating scene. Remember that you are worthy of love and respect, and that true confidence comes from within.

Creating a Positive Mindset. In the world of dating and relationships, having a positive mindset can make all the difference. When you approach dating with a positive attitude, you are more likely to attract positive experiences and outcomes. Creating a positive mindset begins with focusing on the things that bring you joy and fulfillment in life. This could be spending time with loved ones, pursuing hobbies, or practicing self-care activities. By prioritizing your own happiness and well-being, you will naturally exude positivity and attract like-minded individuals into your life.

One of the key aspects of creating a positive mindset is practicing gratitude. Taking time each day to reflect on the things you are grateful for can help shift your perspective and cultivate a sense of abundance. This can be as simple as jotting down a few things you are thankful for in a journal or sharing them with a friend. By focusing on the positive aspects of your life, you will train your brain to see the good in every situation, including your dating experiences.

Another important aspect of creating a positive mindset in the dating scene is letting go of past hurts and disappointments. Holding onto negative emotions from past relationships can cloud your judgment and prevent you from fully embracing new opportunities. By practicing forgiveness and releasing any lingering resentments, you can free yourself from the burden of the past and approach dating with a fresh perspective. This will allow you to be more open and receptive to new connections and experiences.

It is also essential to surround yourself with positive influences and supportive individuals who uplift and encourage you. Whether it's friends, family, or a therapist, having a strong support system can help you maintain a positive mindset during the ups and downs of dating. Seek out people who share your values and beliefs, and who are invested in your happiness and well-being. By nurturing these relationships, you will have a solid foundation of positivity to lean on when faced with challenges in the dating scene.

In conclusion, creating a positive mindset is essential for navigating the dating scene with grace and confidence. By focusing on the things that bring you joy, practicing gratitude, letting go of past hurts, and surrounding yourself with positive influences, you can cultivate a mindset that attracts positive experiences and relationships into your life. Remember, dating is a journey, and having a positive mindset will not only help you enjoy the ride but also lead you to meaningful connections and fulfilling relationships.

Chapter 3
Navigating Online Dating

Choosing the Right Dating Platform. When it comes to dating in the modern world, there are countless options available for meeting new people and potentially finding a romantic partner. One of the most important decisions you will make in your dating journey is choosing the right dating platform for you. With so many options to choose from, it can be overwhelming to know where to start. In this subchapter, we will explore some key factors to consider when selecting a dating platform that aligns with your goals and preferences.

The first step in choosing the right dating platform is to determine what you are looking for in a relationship. Are you seeking a casual fling, a long-term commitment, or something in between? Different dating platforms cater to different relationship goals, so it is important to choose one that aligns with what you are looking for. Some platforms are geared towards hookups and casual encounters, while others are more focused on fostering meaningful connections and long-term relationships.

Another important factor to consider when choosing a dating platform is your comfort level with technology. Some platforms require more technical savvy than others, so it is important to choose one that you feel comfortable using. If you are not comfortable navigating complex apps or websites, you may want to opt for a more user-friendly platform that is easy to use and navigate.

It is also important to consider the demographics of the dating platform you are considering. Different platforms attract different types of users, so it is important to choose one that has a user base that aligns with your preferences. For example, if you are looking for a partner of a specific age group or background, you may want to choose a platform that caters to that demographic.

In addition to considering the features and user base of a dating platform, it is also important to consider the cost. While many dating platforms offer free basic memberships, some may require a paid subscription to access premium features. It is important to weigh the cost of a subscription against the potential benefits of the platform and decide if it is worth the investment for you. By carefully considering these factors, you can choose the right dating platform that aligns with your goals, preferences, and comfort level, setting yourself up for success in the dating world.

Creating an Authentic Profile. In the world of online dating, creating an authentic profile is crucial to finding success in the dating scene. Your profile is often the first impression others will have of you, so it's important to make sure it accurately reflects who you are. When creating your profile, it's essential to be honest and genuine about yourself. It can be tempting to embellish or exaggerate certain aspects of your life, but this will only lead to disappointment and potential distrust from potential matches.

One of the most important aspects of creating an authentic profile is choosing the right photos. Your photos should accurately represent what you look like and showcase your personality. Avoid using heavily filtered or outdated photos, as this can give off a false impression of who you are. Instead, choose photos that show off your interests and hobbies, and make sure to include a mix of close-up and full-body shots.

When writing your profile bio, be sure to highlight your interests, values, and what you're looking for in a partner. Avoid using cliches or generic phrases, as this can make your profile seem unoriginal and uninteresting. Instead, be specific and unique in your descriptions, and don't be afraid to show off your sense of humor or quirks. This will help potential matches get a better sense of who you are and what you're looking for in a relationship.

It's also important to be mindful of the language and tone you use in your profile. Avoid using negative or self-deprecating language, as this can be a turn-off to potential matches. Instead, focus on highlighting your positive attributes and what makes you unique. Remember, the goal of your profile is to attract like-minded individuals who are interested in getting to know the real you.

Overall, creating an authentic profile is essential to finding success in the dating scene. By being honest, genuine, and true to yourself, you'll have a much better chance of attracting potential matches who are truly compatible with you. Remember, the right person will appreciate you for who you are, so don't be afraid to show off your true self in your profile.

Safety Tips for Online Dating. Online dating has become increasingly popular in today's digital age, offering a convenient way to meet new people and potentially find love. However, it is important to prioritize your safety when navigating the world of online dating. Here are some essential safety tips to keep in mind:

First and foremost, trust your instincts. If something feels off or too good to be true, it probably is. Listen to your gut and don't ignore any red flags. If a person you are communicating with online makes you feel uncomfortable or exhibits suspicious behavior, it is best to cut off contact and move on.

When setting up a date with someone you met online, always choose a public place for the first meeting. Avoid private or secluded locations and let a friend or family member know where you will be and who you will be meeting. It is also a good idea to have your own transportation to and from the date to ensure you have a way to leave if needed.

Be cautious about sharing personal information with someone you have just met online. Avoid disclosing sensitive details such as your home address, financial information, or work location until you have established trust and feel comfortable with the person. Keep your communication on the dating platform until you are confident in the person's intentions.

Beware of individuals who try to rush the relationship or pressure you into meeting in person before you are ready. Take your time getting to know someone and communicate openly and honestly about your boundaries and expectations. If someone is not respectful of your wishes, it may be a sign that they are not the right match for you.

Lastly, always prioritize your safety and well-being above all else. If at any point you feel unsafe or threatened by someone you met online, do not hesitate to block them, and report their behavior to the dating platform. Remember that your safety is paramount, and it is important to take proactive steps to protect yourself while navigating the world of online dating.

Chapter 4
Exploring the Digital Dating Landscape

The Modern Romance Revolution. In the 21st century, the landscape of love has been fundamentally transformed by the advent of online dating websites. These platforms have revolutionized how people connect, offering unprecedented access to potential partners. With a plethora of options available, each catering to diverse needs and preferences, understanding the unique features of these platforms is essential for anyone venturing into the world of digital dating.

Online dating has democratized the process of finding a partner, breaking down geographical and social barriers that once limited the dating pool. Individuals can now meet potential matches from across the globe, broadening their horizons and increasing their chances of finding a compatible partner. This shift has not only expanded possibilities but also challenged traditional dating norms, making it possible for people to date more intentionally and selectively.

However, with great possibilities come new challenges. The abundance of choices can sometimes lead to decision fatigue, making it difficult for individuals to commit to a single match. Additionally, the anonymity of online interactions can result in deceptive behaviors, such as catfishing. Despite these challenges, the benefits of online dating far outweigh the drawbacks, offering a powerful tool for those willing to navigate the complexities of digital romance.

Match.com: The Pioneer of Online Dating. Launched in 1995, Match.com is one of the oldest and most well-known online dating websites. It has built a reputation for fostering serious relationships, boasting numerous success stories. Match.com uses a comprehensive algorithm to suggest potential matches based on users' profiles, preferences, and activities on the site. Its extensive database and user-friendly interface make it a reliable choice for those seeking long-term relationships. The platform offers a mix of free and paid features, with the latter providing enhanced search capabilities and detailed compatibility reports.

Match.com's longevity in the industry gives it a significant edge. Over the years, it has accumulated a vast user base, which increases the chances of finding a suitable match. The site caters to a wide demographic, including different age groups, ethnicities, and orientations, ensuring that everyone can find someone who fits their criteria. Additionally, Match.com organizes events and activities for its members, providing opportunities for offline interactions that can enhance the online dating experience.

Despite its many strengths, Match.com is not without its criticisms. Some users find the subscription fees to be relatively high, and there have been occasional complaints about the accuracy of the matching algorithm. However, the platform continuously updates its features and tools, striving to improve user satisfaction. Overall, Match.com remains a formidable player in the online dating industry, particularly for those serious about finding a long-term partner.

eHarmony: Science Meets Love. eHarmony distinguishes itself through its scientific approach to matchmaking. Founded by a clinical psychologist, eHarmony utilizes a detailed personality assessment to pair users based on 32 dimensions of compatibility. This in-depth questionnaire aims to create matches with a higher likelihood of long-term success. While eHarmony requires a subscription for full access, users often find the investment worthwhile due to the platform's focus on serious, committed relationships. Its emphasis on psychological compatibility makes it a popular choice for those looking to build a lasting bond.

The extensive personality test is a cornerstone of eHarmony's approach. By assessing various aspects of a user's personality, including emotional temperament, social style, and cognitive modes, the platform aims to create deeply compatible matches. This scientific method reduces the chances of mismatches and increases the probability of a successful relationship. The focus on compatibility extends beyond superficial traits, delving into core values and beliefs that are crucial for long-term harmony.

While eHarmony's rigorous approach is highly effective for some, it can be time-consuming and may deter those seeking quicker, more casual connections. The detailed sign-up process, coupled with the subscription requirement, means that the platform primarily attracts users who are serious about finding a meaningful relationship. This commitment to quality over quantity has helped eHarmony maintain a strong reputation in the online dating world, particularly among those who value depth and compatibility in their romantic pursuits.

Tinder: The Game Changer. Tinder revolutionized the online dating scene with its introduction in 2012, popularizing the swipe-based matchmaking system. Known for its simplicity and immediate gratification, Tinder appeals to a younger demographic and those seeking more casual relationships. Users swipe right to like and left to pass, with mutual matches allowing for direct messaging. While Tinder initially gained a reputation for fostering hookups, it has since evolved to accommodate a broader range of relationship types. Its user-friendly interface and geolocation features make it a convenient choice for spontaneous connections.

The ease of use and immediacy of Tinder's interface have contributed significantly to its popularity. The app's design encourages quick, intuitive decisions, making the process of finding matches both engaging and addictive. This approach resonates particularly well with younger users who are accustomed to fast-paced, visually driven social media interactions. Additionally, Tinder's geolocation feature allows users to connect with potential matches nearby, facilitating real-time, spontaneous meetups.

However, Tinder's focus on appearance and instant attraction has also drawn criticism. Some argue that the app's design promotes superficiality, with users making snap judgments based solely on photos. This can lead to a lack of depth in connections and may contribute to a culture of casual, short-term relationships. Despite these critiques, Tinder remains one of the most popular dating apps worldwide, continually adapting its features to cater to a diverse user base seeking various types of connections.

Bumble: Empowering Women. Bumble emerged in 2014 with a unique twist on the swipe-based model pioneered by Tinder. On Bumble, women make the first move in heterosexual matches, promoting a sense of empowerment and encouraging respectful interactions. This feature has resonated with many users, contributing to Bumble's rapid growth. The platform also offers modes for finding friends (Bumble BFF) and professional networking (Bumble Bizz), broadening its appeal. Bumble's commitment to fostering a safe and inclusive environment makes it a standout choice for women and those seeking meaningful connections.

Bumble's innovative approach addresses common issues faced by women on dating platforms, such as unsolicited messages and harassment. By giving women control over initiating conversations, Bumble creates a safer and more respectful environment. This empowerment aligns with broader social movements advocating for gender equality and has made Bumble particularly appealing to women seeking a more positive online dating experience.

In addition to its feminist approach, Bumble's versatility sets it apart from other dating apps. The introduction of Bumble BFF and Bumble

Bizz allows users to expand their social and professional networks, making the app a multifunctional platform. These features have broadened Bumble's user base and increased its utility beyond just romantic connections. Whether looking for friendship, professional opportunities, or love, Bumble offers a comprehensive solution that aligns with modern social dynamics.

OkCupid: The Versatile Option. OkCupid is celebrated for its versatility and inclusivity. Launched in 2004, the platform uses a combination of user-generated questions and an algorithm to suggest matches. OkCupid is particularly popular among millennials and members of the LGBTQ+ community due to its progressive approach and comprehensive profile options. The platform offers a range of communication tools and match filters, with both free and premium options available. Its emphasis on compatibility questions and detailed profiles allows users to find matches that align with their values and interests.

One of OkCupid's defining features is its extensive questionnaire, which covers a wide range of topics from lifestyle choices to personal beliefs. Users' answers help the algorithm generate compatibility scores, providing insight into potential matches' compatibility. This detailed approach appeals to those who value deeper connections based on shared values and interests. Additionally, OkCupid's inclusive environment and support for diverse orientations and identities make it a welcoming space for everyone.

Despite its strengths, OkCupid's comprehensive profiles and lengthy questionnaires can be overwhelming for some users. The platform's focus on detailed matching might not appeal to those seeking quick, casual interactions. However, for individuals interested in meaningful relationships and willing to invest time in creating a thorough profile, OkCupid offers a rich and rewarding online dating experience. Its blend of free and premium features ensures accessibility while providing options for enhanced functionality.

Plenty of Fish (POF): Affordability and Accessibility. Plenty of Fish, commonly known as POF, offers a cost-effective solution for online daters. Founded in 2003, POF provides many features for free, making it accessible to a wide audience. The platform includes personality assessments and behavioral matchmaking to enhance the user experience. POF's large user base and extensive search capabilities make it a viable option for those on a budget. While it may lack some of the advanced features of premium sites, its affordability and ease of use continue to attract a diverse range of users.

POF's affordability is a significant draw for users who want to explore online dating without a substantial financial commitment. The platform offers essential features such as messaging, profile browsing, and search filters for free, making it accessible to a broad demographic. Its user base spans various age groups and backgrounds, increasing the likelihood of finding a compatible match. Additionally, POF's personality assessments help refine the matching process, improving the chances of successful connections.

However, the free nature of POF comes with certain trade-offs. The site can sometimes feel cluttered with ads, and the absence of a subscription fee may attract users who are less serious about finding a relationship. Despite these drawbacks, POF's accessibility and extensive user base make it a practical choice for those exploring online dating for the first time or those who prefer not to invest in premium services. Its blend of affordability and functionality ensures it remains a popular option in the online dating landscape.

EliteSingles: For the Highly Educated. EliteSingles caters to professionals and academics seeking serious relationships. The platform targets users with higher education levels and a focus on career success. EliteSingles uses a detailed personality test and an intelligent matchmaking algorithm to connect compatible individuals. Its emphasis on quality over quantity ensures that users are likely to find partners with similar life goals and intellectual interests. Though subscription-based,

EliteSingles' targeted approach and high success rate make it a worthwhile investment for those in search of a sophisticated match.

The detailed personality test used by EliteSingles is designed to assess traits that are crucial for relationship compatibility, such as communication style, values, and preferences. This meticulous approach results in matches that are more likely to share similar life goals and intellectual interests. EliteSingles' focus on a well-educated, professional user base also means that members are more likely to find partners who understand and respect their career ambitions and lifestyle choices.

Despite its benefits, EliteSingles' premium model and targeted demographic can be seen as limiting factors. The subscription fees are high, which may deter users who are not ready to invest financially in their online dating journey. Additionally, the focus on a highly educated, professional user base might exclude individuals who do not fit this criterion but are still looking for serious relationships. Nevertheless, for those who align with EliteSingles' target audience, the platform offers a high-quality, effective matchmaking experience.

Facebook Dating: Social Media Meets Romance. Facebook Dating, launched in 2019, leverages the vast user base and social networking features of Facebook to offer a unique online dating experience. Integrated directly into the Facebook app, Facebook Dating allows users to create a dating profile separate from their main Facebook profile. The platform suggests matches based on shared interests, events, and groups, enhancing the potential for meaningful connections. One of its standout features is the "Secret Crush" option, where users can select up to nine Facebook friends or Instagram followers they are interested in, revealing the match only if the feeling is mutual.

Facebook Dating's integration with the larger Facebook ecosystem offers several advantages. By using existing social connections and interests, the platform can suggest matches with whom users may already have common ground. This approach can make initial conversations more natural and engaging, as users can discuss shared activities or mutual friends. Additionally, the familiarity of the Facebook interface makes the transition to online dating smoother for those new to digital romance.

Despite its innovative features, Facebook Dating faces challenges, particularly concerning privacy and data security. Given Facebook's history with data breaches, some users may be hesitant to trust the platform with their sensitive dating information. However, Facebook Dating has implemented robust privacy controls, ensuring that dating activity is not shared on the main Facebook profile. For those comfortable with these measures, Facebook Dating offers a convenient and integrated way to explore romantic possibilities within their existing social network.

Conclusion: Finding Your Perfect Platform. Navigating the myriad of online dating websites can be daunting, but understanding the unique features and strengths of each platform can help you make an informed choice. Whether you are seeking a long-term relationship, a casual fling, or something in between, there is a platform tailored to your needs. By exploring these options, you can find a digital space that aligns with your goals and preferences, paving the way for meaningful connections in the digital age.

The key to successful online dating lies in selecting the platform that best suits your personal needs and relationship goals. Each site offers distinct features designed to cater to specific demographics and preferences, from Match.com's extensive database to Bumble's women-first approach and eHarmony's scientific matching system. By taking the time to understand these differences, you can maximize your chances of finding a compatible partner and creating a fulfilling relationship.

As you embark on your online dating journey, remember that success often requires patience, openness, and a willingness to explore different options. The digital dating landscape is vast and varied, offering numerous opportunities for connection and companionship. With the right approach and a clear understanding of what each platform offers, you can navigate this landscape with confidence and optimism, ultimately finding the love and partnership you seek.

Chapter 5
Building Healthy Relationships

Establishing Boundaries. Establishing boundaries is a crucial aspect of navigating the dating scene as an adult. Boundaries are guidelines that we set for ourselves and communicate to our partners about what we are comfortable with and what we are not. It is essential to establish boundaries early on in a relationship to ensure that both parties are on the same page and feel respected and valued. Without clear boundaries, misunderstandings and conflicts can arise, leading to potential hurt and disappointment.

One important aspect of establishing boundaries is knowing and understanding your own needs and limits. Take the time to reflect on what you are comfortable with in a relationship, whether it be physical boundaries, emotional boundaries, or time boundaries. Communicate these boundaries to your partner in a clear and respectful manner. Remember, boundaries are not meant to restrict or control your partner, but rather to create a healthy and respectful dynamic in the relationship.

It is also important to listen to your partner's boundaries and respect them. Just as you have your own needs and limits, your partner also has theirs. Be open and receptive to their boundaries, and make sure to honor and respect them. Building trust and mutual respect in a relationship requires both parties to feel heard and understood when it comes to their boundaries.

In addition, boundaries can evolve and change over time. As you grow and learn more about yourself and your partner, your boundaries may shift. It is important to have open and honest communication with your partner about any changes in your boundaries. Keeping the lines of communication open will help ensure that both parties feel secure and respected in the relationship.

Establishing boundaries is a key component of building a healthy and fulfilling relationship. By setting clear boundaries, communicating openly with your partner, and respecting each other's needs and limits, you can create a strong foundation for a successful and loving partnership. Remember, boundaries are not meant to restrict or hinder your relationship, but rather to enhance and strengthen it.

Effective Communication in Relationships. Effective communication is essential in any relationship, whether it be romantic, familial, or friendly. In romantic relationships, effective communication is even more crucial as it forms the foundation for a strong and healthy partnership. Without open and honest communication, misunderstandings can easily arise, leading to conflicts and resentment. Therefore, it is important for adults navigating the dating scene to prioritize effective communication in their relationships.

One key aspect of effective communication in relationships is active listening. This means truly listening to your partner without interrupting or formulating a response in your head while they are speaking. By actively listening, you show your partner that you value their thoughts and feelings, which can strengthen the bond between you. Additionally, active listening can help prevent misunderstandings and conflicts by ensuring that both partners are on the same page.

Another important aspect of effective communication in relationships is being able to express your own thoughts and feelings openly and honestly. It can be tempting to avoid difficult conversations or sweep issues under the rug, but this only leads to pent-up emotions and resentment. By being open and honest with your partner about how you feel, you can address any issues before they escalate and work together to find a resolution that satisfies both parties.

Furthermore, effective communication in relationships involves being able to communicate your needs and boundaries clearly. It is important to understand and respect each other's boundaries in a relationship, and the only way to do so is through open and honest communication. By clearly expressing your needs and boundaries, you can ensure that both you and your partner feel respected and understood, leading to a healthier and more fulfilling relationship.

In conclusion, effective communication is the cornerstone of a successful and fulfilling relationship. By actively listening, expressing your thoughts and feelings openly and honestly, and communicating your needs and boundaries clearly, you can build a strong foundation for a healthy partnership. As adults navigating the dating scene, it is important to prioritize effective communication in your relationships to ensure that they are built on trust, understanding, and respect.

Resolving Conflicts Constructively. Conflicts are a natural part of any relationship, including dating. However, how you handle these conflicts can make a big difference in the overall health and longevity of your relationship. Resolving conflicts constructively is essential for maintaining a strong and healthy connection with your partner. In this sub-chapter, we will explore some strategies for effectively resolving conflicts in a dating relationship.

First and foremost, it's important to approach conflicts with an open mind and a willingness to listen. Avoid getting defensive or shutting down when your partner brings up an issue. Instead, try to see things from their perspective and validate their feelings. Active listening is key to resolving conflicts constructively, so make sure to give your partner your full attention and avoid interrupting them.

Communication is another crucial aspect of resolving conflicts constructively. Be honest and open about your feelings and concerns, but also be respectful and considerate of your partner's feelings. Use "I" statements to express how you feel without placing blame on your partner. Avoid using hurtful language or resorting to personal attacks during conflicts. Instead, focus on finding common ground and working together to find a solution that satisfies both parties.

Finding a compromise is often the best way to resolve conflicts in a dating relationship. Both partners should be willing to make concessions and find a middle ground that meets both of their needs. Remember that relationships are a partnership, and it's important to work together as a team to overcome challenges and disagreements. Compromise requires both parties to be flexible and willing to make adjustments for the greater good of the relationship.

Finally, it's important to practice forgiveness and let go of grudges after conflicts have been resolved. Holding onto resentment and anger can breed further conflicts and damage the trust in your relationship. Instead, focus on moving forward and learning from the conflict to strengthen your bond with your partner. Remember that conflicts are a natural part of any relationship and resolving them constructively can help you grow closer and deepen your connection with your partner.

Chapter 6
Red Flags to Watch Out For

Recognizing Manipulative Behaviors. In the world of dating and relationships, it is important to be aware of manipulative behaviors that may be present in your partner. Manipulative behaviors can range from subtle to overt, but they all have one thing in common - they are designed to control and manipulate the other person for their own gain. Recognizing these behaviors early on can help you protect yourself and maintain a healthy relationship.

One common manipulative behavior to watch out for is gaslighting. Gaslighting is a form of emotional manipulation where the manipulator makes the other person doubt their own feelings, thoughts, and perceptions. They may twist the truth, deny things they have said or done, and make you feel like you are going crazy. If you find yourself constantly questioning your own reality in a relationship, it may be a sign of gaslighting.

Another manipulative behavior to be aware of is guilt-tripping. Guilt-tripping is when someone uses your feelings of guilt or obligation to get what they want. They may make you feel bad for not doing something they want or manipulate you into doing things you don't want to do by making you feel guilty. If you find yourself constantly feeling guilty or apologizing for things in your relationship, it may be a sign of guilt-tripping.

Manipulative behaviors can also include passive-aggressive actions. Passive-aggressive behavior is when someone expresses their anger or resentment in a subtle or indirect way. They may give you the silent treatment, make snide remarks, or intentionally forget to do things they promised. If you find yourself feeling frustrated or confused by your partner's behavior, it may be a sign of passive-aggressiveness.

It is important to remember that manipulative behaviors are not healthy or normal in a relationship. If you recognize any of these behaviors in your partner, it is important to address them and set boundaries. Communication is key in any relationship, so make sure to have open and honest conversations about how you are feeling and what you need from the other person. Remember, you deserve to be in a relationship where you are respected and treated with kindness and understanding.

Identifying Signs of Emotional Abuse. Emotional abuse is a serious issue that can often go unnoticed in relationships. It can be subtle and manipulative, making it difficult to identify. However, it is important to be able to recognize the signs of emotional abuse in order to protect yourself and maintain a healthy relationship. In this sub-chapter, we will explore some common signs of emotional abuse and provide guidance on how to address it.

One of the key signs of emotional abuse is constant criticism and put-downs. If your partner is constantly belittling you, making you feel inadequate or unworthy, this is a clear red flag. Other signs include controlling behavior, such as monitoring your every move, isolating you from friends and family, or making all the decisions in the relationship. Gaslighting is another common form of emotional abuse, where your partner manipulates you into questioning your own reality and sanity.

It is important to trust your instincts and pay attention to how you feel in the relationship. If you constantly feel anxious, depressed, or on edge around your partner, this may be a sign of emotional abuse. Additionally, if you find yourself walking on eggshells to avoid conflict or upsetting your partner, this is another red flag. Remember, you deserve to be treated with respect and kindness in a relationship.

If you suspect that you are experiencing emotional abuse, it is important to reach out for support. Talk to a trusted friend or family member about your concerns or consider seeking help from a therapist or counselor. It can be difficult to confront your partner about their behavior, but it is important to set boundaries and advocate for yourself. Remember, you deserve to be in a healthy and loving relationship.

In conclusion, emotional abuse can have serious consequences on your mental and emotional well-being. By being able to identify the signs of emotional abuse, you can take steps to protect yourself and seek help if needed. Remember, you deserve to be treated with respect and kindness in all your relationships. Take care of yourself and prioritize your own well-being.

Trusting Your Instincts. Trusting your instincts is a crucial skill to have when navigating the dating scene. As adults, we have a wealth of life experience that can help guide us in making decisions about who to date and how to approach potential relationships. Our instincts are like a built-in compass, pointing us in the right direction and helping us avoid potential pitfalls along the way.

When it comes to dating, our instincts can often tell us more than we realize. We may have a gut feeling about someone we meet, or a sense of unease that tells us something isn't quite right. It's important to listen to these feelings and trust our instincts, even if we can't always explain why we feel a certain way. Our instincts are often our subconscious mind picking up on subtle cues and signals that our conscious mind may not be aware of.

Trusting our instincts can also help protect us from potential harm or danger. If we get a bad feeling about someone we're dating, it's important to listen to that feeling and take it seriously. Our instincts are there to help keep us safe and ignoring them can lead to dangerous situations. By trusting our instincts, we can avoid getting involved with people who may not have our best interests at heart.

It's also important to remember that our instincts are not infallible. While they can be a valuable tool in the dating scene, they are not always right. It's important to balance our instincts with rational thinking and careful consideration. We should take the time to get to know someone before making any major decisions about dating them, and not rely solely on our gut feelings.

In conclusion, trusting our instincts is an important skill to have when navigating the dating scene as adults. Our instincts can help guide us in making decisions about who to date and how to approach potential relationships. By listening to our instincts, we can protect ourselves from harm and make better choices about who to let into our lives. Remember to trust your gut, but also take the time to get to know someone before making any major decisions.

Chapter 7
Embracing Singlehood

Rediscovering *Your Passions.* Embracing singlehood is an opportunity to reconnect with your passions and interests, free from the compromises that often accompany relationships. This period allows you to explore hobbies you may have neglected, dive into new activities, or rediscover old ones with renewed enthusiasm. Whether it's painting, hiking, learning a new language, or traveling, singlehood offers the gift of time and freedom to pursue these interests without external obligations. By engaging in activities that genuinely excite you, you not only enrich your life but also build a deeper understanding of what makes you happy.

Rediscovering your passions can lead to personal growth and increased self-awareness. As you invest time in activities you love, you cultivate skills, expand your knowledge, and boost your confidence. This process fosters a sense of fulfillment that comes from within, independent of external validation. Embracing your interests wholeheartedly can transform your perspective on singlehood from one of solitude to one of opportunity, helping you appreciate the value of your own company and the joy that comes from doing what you love.

Cultivating Self-Compassion. Cultivating self-compassion is a crucial aspect of embracing singlehood. Often, people are their harshest critics, holding themselves to unrealistic standards and feeling unworthy if they don't meet them. Singlehood provides a chance to practice kindness towards yourself, to forgive your mistakes, and to understand that imperfection is a part of being human. By treating yourself with the same empathy and understanding you would offer a friend, you create a supportive inner dialogue that can significantly improve your emotional well-being.

Self-compassion involves recognizing your struggles without judgment and allowing yourself to experience and process your emotions. This practice helps build resilience and fosters a healthier, more balanced relationship with yourself. In a state of singlehood, you have the space to focus on your mental and emotional health, learning to accept and love yourself unconditionally. This foundation of self-compassion not only enhances your current life experience but also prepares you for healthier, more fulfilling relationships in the future.

Setting Personal Goals. Singlehood is an excellent time to set personal goals and work towards them with determination. Without the distractions or compromises that come with a relationship, you can focus on what you truly want to achieve. Whether it's advancing in your career, pursuing further education, or improving your physical health, setting clear, attainable goals gives you direction and purpose. This period allows you to invest in yourself and lay the groundwork for future successes.

Achieving personal goals during singlehood can be incredibly empowering. Each milestone reached boosts your confidence and reinforces your sense of self-efficacy. The process of working towards and accomplishing goals teaches you valuable lessons about perseverance, discipline, and self-motivation. Moreover, it shows that you are capable of creating a fulfilling and meaningful life on your own terms. This sense of accomplishment enhances your overall well-being and prepares you to enter future relationships as a whole and self-assured individual.

Building a Strong Support System. While singlehood is a time for self-discovery and personal growth, it's also important to build and maintain a strong support system. Friends and family provide essential emotional support, offering different perspectives and helping you navigate life's challenges. Investing in these relationships can bring a sense of belonging and community, reducing feelings of loneliness and isolation. Spending quality time with loved ones, sharing experiences, and creating new memories enriches your life and reinforces the importance of connection.

A strong support system also includes seeking out new social opportunities. Joining clubs, volunteering, or participating in group activities can introduce you to like-minded individuals and broaden your social network. These connections not only provide companionship but also inspire you and challenge you to grow. Surrounding yourself with positive influences and people who encourage your personal development can significantly enhance your singlehood experience, making it a period of rich social and emotional fulfillment.

Embracing Solitude. Embracing solitude is an integral part of building a relationship with yourself. Many people fear being alone, associating it with loneliness or a lack of social approval. However, solitude can be a powerful tool for introspection and self-improvement. Taking time to be alone allows you to reflect on your life, understand your thoughts and feelings, and gain clarity on your desires and aspirations. It's a chance to disconnect from external distractions and focus entirely on your inner world.

Solitude also promotes creativity and innovation. Without the constant input and opinions of others, you can think more freely and deeply. This quiet time can lead to new ideas, insights, and solutions to problems. By learning to enjoy your own company, you cultivate a sense of inner peace and contentment that is independent of your external circumstances. Embracing solitude strengthens your self-reliance and helps you appreciate the value of spending time alone, making you more resilient and self-assured.

Nurturing Self-Love. Nurturing self-love is the cornerstone of a healthy relationship with yourself. Self-love goes beyond self-compassion; it involves recognizing your worth and treating yourself with the same respect and care you would give to someone you love deeply. This means prioritizing your needs, setting healthy boundaries, and engaging in self-care practices that nourish your body, mind, and soul. Singlehood provides the perfect opportunity to develop and deepen this self-love.

Self-love is an ongoing practice that requires daily commitment and mindfulness. It's about celebrating your achievements, forgiving your failures, and always striving to be the best version of yourself. By nurturing self-love, you create a strong, positive foundation that supports your overall well-being. This self-assuredness and inner strength will not only make your singlehood more fulfilling but also enhance your future relationships, as you will enter them with a clear sense of self-worth and a healthy perspective on love and partnership.

Finding Joy in Independence. Independence is one of the most liberating aspects of singlehood. It allows you to make decisions solely based on your preferences, without needing to consider a partner's input. This autonomy enables you to live life on your own terms, from choosing where to live and work to how you spend your free time. Embracing this independence can lead to a deeper understanding of your own needs and desires, fostering a sense of empowerment and control over your life.

Finding joy in independence also involves financial freedom and the ability to manage your resources according to your priorities. This period allows you to focus on financial literacy, budgeting, and investing in your future. By gaining control over your finances, you build a stable foundation that supports your long-term goals. This financial independence further enhances your sense of self-reliance and security, making your singlehood a period of significant personal and economic growth.

Enhancing Emotional Intelligence. Singlehood provides a unique opportunity to enhance your emotional intelligence, which is crucial for personal and professional success. Emotional intelligence involves understanding and managing your own emotions, as well as recognizing and influencing the emotions of others. During this time, you can focus on developing skills such as empathy, self-regulation, and effective communication. These skills improve your relationships with others and your ability to navigate social situations with confidence and grace.

Enhancing your emotional intelligence also involves reflecting on past relationships and learning from them. By analyzing your emotional responses and understanding the triggers behind them, you gain insights into your behavior patterns and how they impact your interactions. This self-awareness helps you build healthier, more meaningful connections in the future. Additionally, high emotional intelligence contributes to better mental health, as you become more adept at handling stress and managing conflicts constructively.

Prioritizing Physical Health. Singlehood is an ideal time to prioritize your physical health. Without the added responsibilities of a relationship, you can focus on establishing and maintaining healthy habits that contribute to your overall well-being. Regular exercise, balanced nutrition, and adequate sleep are fundamental components of a healthy lifestyle. By dedicating time to these activities, you improve your physical fitness, boost your energy levels, and enhance your mental clarity.

Focusing on physical health also involves preventative care and listening to your body's needs. Scheduling regular medical check-ups, addressing any health concerns promptly, and adopting a proactive approach to wellness can prevent future health issues. This commitment to your physical well-being reinforces the importance of self-care and demonstrates a deep respect for your body. As you cultivate these healthy habits, you not only feel better physically but also gain a sense of accomplishment and self-discipline that benefits all areas of your life.

Exploring Personal Identity. Singlehood offers the perfect environment to explore and define your personal identity. Free from the influence of a partner, you have the space to delve into who you are at your core. This exploration involves understanding your values, beliefs, and what truly matters to you. By engaging in introspective activities such as journaling, meditation, or seeking therapy, you can uncover aspects of your identity that may have been overshadowed by previous relationships.

Exploring your personal identity also includes understanding your strengths and areas for growth. This self-knowledge empowers you to make decisions that align with your authentic self, fostering a sense of integrity and self-respect. As you become more attuned to your true self, you build a solid foundation for your future, ensuring that any relationships you enter into will complement rather than compromise your individuality. This journey of self-discovery ultimately leads to a deeper, more fulfilling connection with yourself.

Chapter 8
Nurturing Long-Term Relationships

K*eeping the Spark Alive.* Keeping the spark alive in a relationship is essential for maintaining a healthy and fulfilling connection with your partner. In the hustle and bustle of everyday life, it can be easy to let the romance and excitement fade away. However, with some effort and intentionality, you can keep the spark alive and continue to grow closer with your significant other.

One way to keep the spark alive is to make time for regular date nights. Whether it's going out to a fancy dinner, taking a stroll in the park, or simply cuddling up on the couch to watch a movie, setting aside dedicated time for just the two of you can help strengthen your bond and remind you why you fell in love in the first place. Date nights allow you to focus on each other without distractions and rekindle the romance in your relationship.

Another important aspect of keeping the spark alive is to communicate openly and honestly with your partner. Share your thoughts, feelings, and desires with each other regularly to ensure that you are on the same page and continue to grow together. Expressing appreciation and gratitude for your partner can also go a long way in keeping the spark alive. A simple "thank you" or a heartfelt compliment can show your partner that you value and cherish them, strengthening your connection and bringing you closer together.

Physical intimacy is also a key component of keeping the spark alive in a relationship. Make time for regular physical affection, whether it's holding hands, hugging, kissing, or being intimate. Physical touch releases feel-good hormones like oxytocin and dopamine, which can increase feelings of closeness and connection between you and your partner. Don't underestimate the power of a simple touch in keeping the spark alive in your relationship.

Lastly, don't forget to have fun and laugh together. Laughter is a powerful tool for strengthening relationships and creating lasting bonds. Find ways to inject humor and playfulness into your relationship, whether it's telling jokes, watching a funny movie, or going on adventures together. By prioritizing laughter and fun in your relationship, you can keep the spark alive and continue to grow closer with your partner for years to come.

Balancing Individuality and Togetherness. In any romantic relationship, it is essential to strike a balance between maintaining your individuality and fostering togetherness. This delicate equilibrium is crucial for the success and longevity of the partnership. It is important to remember that you are two separate individuals coming together to form a strong, supportive unit.

One way to ensure that you are balancing individuality and togetherness is by setting boundaries. These boundaries can help each partner maintain their sense of self while also respecting the needs and boundaries of their significant other. Communication is key in establishing and maintaining these boundaries, so make sure to have open and honest conversations about your needs and expectations.

Finding common interests and activities to enjoy together can also help strengthen the bond between partners while still allowing each individual to maintain their own interests and hobbies. By spending quality time together engaging in activities you both enjoy, you can create shared experiences that will bring you closer together while still honoring your individual interests.

It is also important to prioritize self-care and personal growth in a relationship. Taking care of yourself and pursuing your own personal goals and interests will not only make you a happier, more fulfilled individual, but it will also benefit your relationship. When both partners are focused on their own personal growth and well-being, they are better equipped to support each other in the relationship.

Ultimately, finding the right balance between individuality and togetherness in a relationship requires effort and compromise from both partners. By being mindful of each other's needs and boundaries, communicating openly and honestly, and prioritizing self-care and personal growth, you can create a strong and healthy partnership that allows both individuals to thrive both as individuals and as a couple.

Growing Together as a Couple. In any relationship, growth is essential. As a couple, it is important to grow together in order to strengthen your bond and build a lasting connection. This sub-chapter will explore the ways in which couples can grow together and navigate the ups and downs of their relationship.

One key aspect of growing together as a couple is communication. Open and honest communication is vital to a healthy relationship. It is important to express your thoughts and feelings to your partner in a respectful and constructive manner. By communicating effectively, you can work through any challenges that may arise and strengthen your relationship in the process.

Another way to grow together as a couple is to set goals and work towards them as a team. Whether it's saving for a vacation, buying a house, or starting a family, setting goals together can help you stay connected and focused on the future. By working towards a common goal, you can build a sense of unity and shared purpose in your relationship.

It is also important to make time for each other and prioritize your relationship. In the hustle and bustle of daily life, it can be easy to neglect your relationship and take each other for granted. Make an effort to spend quality time together, whether it's going on a date night, taking a weekend trip, or simply enjoying a quiet evening at home. By making your relationship a priority, you can strengthen your bond and grow closer as a couple.

Finally, growing together as a couple also means supporting each other through the good times and the bad. Life is full of ups and downs, and it's important to be there for each other through it all. By offering each other love, support, and encouragement, you can weather any storm and come out stronger on the other side. By growing together as a couple, you can build a solid foundation for a lasting and fulfilling relationship.

Chapter 9
Navigating Marriage

Entering *a Marital Contract.* Marriage is often seen as the ultimate commitment in a romantic relationship, symbolizing a partnership built on love, trust, and mutual respect. However, maintaining a healthy marriage requires continuous effort, understanding, and adaptation. In this chapter, we will explore various facets of marriage relationships, including communication, conflict resolution, intimacy, and the impact of external factors such as career and family dynamics.

Communication: The Foundation of a Strong Marriage. Effective communication is the cornerstone of a healthy marriage. It involves not only talking but also listening and understanding your partner's perspective. Active listening means paying full attention to your partner when they speak and showing empathy towards their feelings and thoughts. Open and honest dialogue is essential; sharing your thoughts and feelings openly, and encouraging your partner to do the same, fosters trust and strengthens your bond. Additionally, non-verbal communication, such as body language, facial expressions, and tone of voice, significantly impacts your partner's perception of your message, so being mindful of these aspects is crucial.

Moreover, making time for regular check-ins can significantly enhance your communication. Setting aside time each week to discuss your feelings, concerns, and aspirations helps maintain an open line of communication. This practice can prevent misunderstandings and ensure that both partners feel heard and valued. Effective communication also involves being patient and avoiding the urge to interrupt or jump to conclusions. By fostering an environment where both partners can express themselves freely, you build a strong foundation for your marriage.

Conflict Resolution: Turning Challenges into Growth Opportunities. Disagreements are inevitable in any relationship, but how you handle them can make a difference. Staying calm and respectful when approaching conflicts helps maintain a constructive atmosphere and shows respect for your partner's viewpoint, even if you disagree. Seeking compromise involves finding solutions that satisfy both parties, ensuring that both partners feel heard and valued. Taking time-outs when emotions run high can prevent escalation and allow for more rational problem-solving, creating opportunities for growth and understanding within the relationship.

Additionally, learning to view conflicts as opportunities for growth can transform your approach to disagreements. By understanding that conflicts are a natural part of any relationship, you can approach them with a problem-solving mindset rather than viewing them as threats to your marriage. Developing conflict resolution skills, such as active listening, empathy, and negotiation, can help you and your partner navigate disagreements more effectively. Over time, successfully resolving conflicts can strengthen your bond and enhance your mutual respect and understanding.

Intimacy: Maintaining Emotional and Physical Connection. Intimacy goes beyond physical closeness; it encompasses emotional and intellectual connections as well. Spending meaningful time together, engaging in activities you both enjoy, strengthens your bond, and creates shared experiences. Regularly expressing physical affection, such as hugging, kissing, and holding hands, reinforces your emotional connection. Being emotionally supportive, offering a listening ear, a shoulder to lean on, and unwavering support during both good times and bad, is essential for maintaining deep intimacy in your marriage.

Building intimacy also involves being vulnerable with each other. Sharing your fears, dreams, and insecurities can deepen your emotional connection and foster a sense of trust and safety in your relationship. Intimacy requires effort and intentionality, so make it a priority to regularly check in with each other on an emotional level. Additionally, maintaining a sense of playfulness and fun in your relationship can help keep the spark alive. Whether it's through shared hobbies, spontaneous adventures, or simple acts of kindness, finding ways to connect on a deeper level will strengthen your marriage.

Balancing Career and Family: Navigating External Pressures. Balancing career aspirations and family life can be challenging, but it is essential for a harmonious marriage. Setting priorities and allocating time accordingly ensures that both career and family needs are met without compromising your relationship. Supporting each other's goals by encouraging and celebrating successes while providing comfort during setbacks fosters a strong partnership. Shared responsibilities in household and childcare duties reduce stress and prevent resentment, promoting cooperation and teamwork.

Finding balance also requires open communication about your expectations and boundaries. Discussing your career goals and family plans helps align your efforts and ensures that both partners are on the same page. Flexibility is key, as life circumstances can change, requiring adjustments to your plans. Being adaptable and willing to renegotiate roles and responsibilities as needed can help maintain harmony in your marriage. Remember to celebrate your achievements, both individually and as a couple, to reinforce your mutual support and commitment.

Financial Harmony: Money Matters in Marriage. Financial issues are a common source of stress in marriages, and developing a shared approach to money management can alleviate tension. Being transparent about your financial situation, including income, debts, and spending habits, builds trust and prevents misunderstandings. Joint financial planning, creating a budget, and setting financial goals together ensure that both partners are on the same page and working towards common objectives. While joint planning is crucial, respecting each other's individual spending preferences and finding a balance that works for both is also important.

Creating a financial plan that reflects your shared values and goals can strengthen your partnership. Regularly reviewing your financial situation and making adjustments as needed helps keep your finances on track. Establishing an emergency fund and saving for future goals, such as buying a home or retirement, can provide a sense of security and shared purpose. Financial harmony also involves being supportive and understanding during financial challenges, such as job loss or unexpected expenses. By working together to navigate these challenges, you build resilience and trust in your marriage.

Dealing with External Influences: Family, Friends, and Society. External influences can impact your marriage and managing them effectively is crucial. Establishing boundaries with extended family and friends protects your marriage from undue interference. Presenting a united front when dealing with external pressures reinforces your partnership and reduces external conflict. While being aware of societal expectations is necessary, prioritizing what works best for your relationship and tailoring your marriage to your unique needs and values is key to maintaining harmony.

Managing external influences also involves setting expectations with your extended family and friends. Communicate your boundaries clearly and consistently to prevent misunderstandings and ensure that your marriage remains a priority. When societal expectations conflict with your values or goals, have open discussions with your partner about how to navigate these pressures. Support each other in resisting external pressures that do not align with your relationship's needs. By prioritizing your marriage and making decisions together, you can maintain a strong and united front against external influences.

Growth and Change: Embracing Evolution in Your Marriage. Marriage is a dynamic relationship that evolves over time. Embracing growth and change is essential to keep your marriage vibrant. Being adaptable and open to new circumstances allows your marriage to thrive despite life's unpredictability. Investing in continuous learning and growing together by attending workshops, reading books, and seeking advice enhances your relationship skills. Recognizing and celebrating important milestones in your marriage reinforces your commitment and creates lasting memories.

Embracing change also involves being open to personal growth and self-improvement. Encourage each other to pursue new interests, hobbies, and career opportunities. Supporting each other's individual growth can enhance your relationship and bring new dimensions to your marriage. Regularly revisiting and updating your shared goals and dreams helps keep your relationship dynamic and aligned with your evolving values. By viewing change as an opportunity for growth rather than a threat, you can foster a resilient and adaptable marriage that stands the test of time.

Parenting: Raising Children as a Team. Parenting can be a significant source of both joy and stress in a marriage. Raising children together requires teamwork and a united approach. Consistent parenting styles provide a stable environment for your children and supporting each other in your roles as parents through open communication about challenges and triumphs strengthens your partnership. Remember to prioritize your relationship as a couple, even while focusing on your children, as a strong marriage provides a solid foundation for your family.

Effective co-parenting involves regularly discussing and aligning on parenting strategies and decisions. Make time to talk about your children's needs, development, and any concerns you may have. Being united in your approach helps provide consistency and security for your children. Additionally, share the responsibilities of parenting to avoid burnout and ensure that both partners feel equally involved. Taking time for yourselves as a couple, away from parenting duties, can help you reconnect and maintain the health of your marriage.

Maintaining Individuality: Balancing Togetherness and Personal Space. While togetherness is important, maintaining individuality within a marriage is equally crucial. Pursuing personal interests outside of the relationship fosters personal growth and fulfillment. Understanding and respecting each other's need for personal space and alone time contribute to a balanced relationship. Celebrating each other's achievements and independence supports both partners' personal and collective goals, reinforcing the strength of your marriage.

Balancing individuality and togetherness requires open communication about your needs and boundaries. Encourage each other to pursue activities and hobbies that bring joy and satisfaction. Respecting each other's need for alone time can help prevent feelings of suffocation or dependency. Additionally, celebrate and support each other's personal growth and achievements. By fostering an environment that values both individual and shared experiences, you create a healthy and dynamic relationship that allows both partners to thrive.

Health and Well-Being: Supporting Each Other's Physical and Mental Health. Supporting each other's health and well-being is vital for a happy marriage. Encouraging and supporting each other in making healthy lifestyle choices, such as regular exercise, balanced nutrition, and sufficient rest, promotes physical health. Being mindful of each other's mental health and offering support during times of stress, while seeking professional help if needed, ensures that both partners maintain their well-being. Setting and pursuing shared health goals together, such as cooking healthy meals or exercising, can strengthen your bond.

Fostering a healthy lifestyle together involves creating routines and habits that support your physical and mental well-being. Engage in activities that you both enjoy, such as hiking, cooking, or meditation, to maintain a healthy balance. Pay attention to each other's stress levels and emotional needs and be proactive in offering support and encouragement. Seeking professional help when needed, whether for physical health issues or mental health concerns, demonstrates your commitment to each other's well-being. By prioritizing health together, you build a foundation for a long, happy, and healthy life.

Romance and Fun: Keeping the Spark Alive. Maintaining romance and fun in your marriage is essential for long-term happiness. Regularly scheduling date nights or special outings helps keep the romance alive and allows you to reconnect and enjoy each other's company. Surprising your partner with small gestures of love and appreciation can reignite passion and show that you care. Engaging in new and exciting activities together creates lasting memories and strengthens your bond, keeping your relationship vibrant and joyful.

Continuing to court each other even after years of marriage can rekindle the spark and keep your relationship exciting. Plan surprises, give thoughtful gifts, or simply spend quality time together doing something you both love. Keeping the element of surprise and spontaneity alive adds excitement to your marriage. Additionally, finding ways to laugh and have fun together helps reduce stress and keeps the relationship light-hearted and enjoyable. By actively nurturing romance and fun, you create a vibrant and fulfilling partnership.

A successful marriage is built on a foundation of strong communication, effective conflict resolution, deep intimacy, and mutual support. By navigating the complexities of career, family, finances, and external influences, you can cultivate a resilient and fulfilling partnership. Embrace growth and change, and continuously invest in your relationship to ensure it remains a source of joy and strength throughout your life together.

Chapter 10
Navigating Same-Sex Relationships

Understanding the Landscape of Same-Sex Relationships. Same-sex relationships have long been a part of human history, yet the recognition and acceptance of these relationships have significantly evolved over recent decades. As societal norms have shifted, so too has the understanding and appreciation of the unique dynamics that characterize same-sex relationships. Embracing these relationships involves understanding their specific challenges and joys, and how they compare and contrast with heterosexual partnerships.

The journey towards acceptance and legal recognition of same-sex relationships has been a rocky path, marked by both significant victories and persistent struggles. In many parts of the world, same-sex couples now enjoy the same legal rights and social acceptance as their heterosexual counterparts. However, this is not universal, and even in progressive regions, same-sex couples may still face unique challenges and prejudices. Understanding this landscape is crucial for anyone navigating or supporting same-sex relationships.

Additionally, the cultural and historical contexts of same-sex relationships provide a richer understanding of their current status. In various cultures, same-sex relationships were historically viewed differently, sometimes revered and at other times condemned. Today, media representation and public discourse play crucial roles in shaping societal attitudes. By examining these historical and cultural shifts, we gain insight into the evolving nature of same-sex relationships and the ongoing efforts to achieve equality and acceptance.

The Unique Dynamics of Same-Sex Relationships. Same-sex relationships, like all relationships, are built on a foundation of love, trust, and mutual respect. However, they often encompass unique dynamics that stem from shared experiences and societal pressures. For instance, same-sex couples may find themselves navigating the complexities of coming out, dealing with internalized homophobia, or facing discrimination from family, friends, or society at large.

One significant aspect of same-sex relationships is the sense of shared understanding and empathy that partners can offer each other. This mutual understanding can create a profound bond, as both individuals often share similar life experiences, from growing up feeling different to facing discrimination. This can lead to a deep emotional connection and a strong sense of solidarity within the relationship.

Furthermore, same-sex relationships can challenge traditional gender roles and expectations. Without predefined gender roles, partners have the flexibility to define their own roles and responsibilities within the relationship. This can lead to a more equitable division of labor and a deeper understanding of each other's strengths and needs. However, it also requires open communication and negotiation to ensure that both partners feel valued and supported.

Communication and Conflict Resolution. Effective communication is the cornerstone of any healthy relationship, and it is particularly vital in same-sex relationships, where external pressures can sometimes exacerbate internal conflicts. Open and honest communication helps partners navigate their unique challenges and ensures that both individuals feel heard and understood.

Conflict resolution in same-sex relationships often involves addressing not only personal disagreements but also external factors such as societal discrimination or family rejection. It is essential for partners to develop strategies to support each other and address these external pressures together. This might involve seeking counseling, joining support groups, or simply creating a safe space where both partners feel valued and protected.

In addition to these strategies, it's important for partners to regularly check in with each other and discuss their feelings and experiences. This ongoing dialogue can help prevent misunderstandings and build a stronger connection. Utilizing tools like couples therapy, mindfulness practices, and conflict resolution workshops can provide additional support and skills to enhance communication and strengthen the relationship.

Legal and Social Considerations. The legal recognition of same-sex marriages and relationships varies widely around the world, impacting the rights and protections available to couples. In many countries, same-sex marriage is now legal, granting couples the same legal rights as heterosexual married couples, including inheritance rights, adoption rights, and tax benefits. However, in other regions, same-sex relationships may still be illegal or lack legal recognition, presenting significant challenges for couples.

Navigating the legal landscape requires awareness and, in some cases, legal assistance to ensure that both partners' rights are protected. This might involve understanding local laws, seeking legal counsel, and advocating for equal rights. Additionally, social acceptance plays a critical role in the well-being of same-sex couples. Support from family, friends, and the broader community can significantly impact the quality of life and mental health of individuals in same-sex relationships.

Legal challenges can also affect everyday aspects of life, such as healthcare decisions, parenting rights, and property ownership. Couples may need to create legal documents like powers of attorney, wills, and cohabitation agreements to protect their rights and interests. Staying informed about changes in laws and policies is crucial for safeguarding the relationship and ensuring that both partners are prepared for any legal contingencies that may arise.

Building and Maintaining Healthy Same-Sex Relationships. Building a healthy same-sex relationship involves the same principles as any other relationship: love, respect, communication, and commitment. However, same-sex couples may also need to navigate additional layers of complexity related to societal attitudes and legal recognition.

Creating a supportive and inclusive environment is crucial. This includes fostering a network of supportive friends and family, seeking out LGBTQ+ friendly spaces and communities, and advocating for acceptance and equality. Self-care and mental health are also vital components, as same-sex couples may face unique stressors that can impact their well-being.

In addition to external support, maintaining a healthy same-sex relationship requires both partners to prioritize each other and their relationship. This can involve regular date nights, shared hobbies, and continual personal growth. Celebrating milestones and achievements together, while also navigating challenges hand in hand, strengthens the bond and creates a resilient partnership. Couples can also benefit from resources such as relationship books, workshops, and retreats designed specifically for same-sex couples.

Celebrating Love in All Its Forms. Navigating same-sex relationships and marriage involves a blend of understanding unique dynamics, effective communication, legal awareness, and creating a supportive environment. Despite the challenges, same-sex relationships offer the opportunity for deep, empathetic connections and the celebration of love in its purest form. By embracing these relationships with openness and respect, we can move towards a society that values and celebrates love in all its diverse expressions.

Ultimately, the journey of a same-sex relationship is one of resilience, courage, and joy. It is a testament to the enduring power of love to overcome obstacles and create lasting connections. By celebrating these relationships and advocating for equality, we contribute to a world where love is recognized and honored in all its forms, paving the way for future generations to experience the freedom and fulfillment of being true to themselves.

Chapter 11
Balancing Hearts and Careers

The *Allure of Workplace Romance.* The workplace, a domain where individuals spend a significant portion of their lives, often becomes a fertile ground for romantic connections. Shared goals, collaborative projects, and the camaraderie of team dynamics can create a unique bond between colleagues. The allure of workplace romance is undeniable, driven by proximity and the natural human inclination towards companionship. However, intertwining professional and personal lives can lead to a complex web of challenges and opportunities.

These relationships can blossom naturally as coworkers share both triumphs and challenges in their professional roles. This shared experience often fosters a deep sense of understanding and mutual respect, which can evolve into a romantic connection. The familiarity and comfort of working closely together can accelerate the bonding process, creating an intimate partnership grounded in shared experiences and goals.

However, the complexity of workplace romances cannot be underestimated. The blending of personal and professional roles requires a heightened level of emotional intelligence and self-awareness. Couples must navigate the fine line between personal affection and professional conduct, ensuring that their relationship enhances rather than detracts from their work environment.

The Pros and Cons of Mixing Business with Pleasure. Engaging in a romantic relationship at work comes with its own set of advantages and disadvantages. On one hand, dating a coworker can enhance job satisfaction and foster a supportive environment. Having a partner who understands the intricacies of your job can be a source of comfort and motivation. On the other hand, workplace romances can blur professional boundaries, leading to potential conflicts of interest and perceptions of favoritism.

A significant advantage of workplace relationships is the built-in support system. Partners who share the same work environment can offer each other unique insights and empathetic support that external partners might struggle to provide. This can result in increased job satisfaction and a more positive outlook on work-related challenges.

Conversely, the potential for conflicts of interest is a serious consideration. Perceptions of favoritism can undermine team morale and lead to resentment among coworkers. Additionally, if the relationship encounters difficulties, it can create tension and discomfort not just for the couple but for the entire team. Balancing these dynamics requires careful consideration and proactive management.

Establishing Boundaries. One of the most critical aspects of a successful workplace romance is the establishment of clear boundaries. It is essential to separate professional responsibilities from personal interactions to prevent conflicts and maintain productivity. Couples should avoid public displays of affection and ensure that their relationship does not interfere with their duties or create discomfort for their colleagues.

Setting clear boundaries helps maintain a professional atmosphere and ensures that personal matters do not spill over into the workplace. This involves agreeing on what is appropriate behavior during work hours and within the office setting. By doing so, couples can demonstrate respect for their colleagues and the professional environment.

Moreover, it's important for couples to have a strategy for managing disagreements. Keeping conflicts or personal issues out of the workplace can prevent unnecessary drama and maintain a positive work environment. Regularly revisiting and adjusting these boundaries as the relationship evolves can help both partners stay aligned and maintain a healthy balance.

Handling Disclosure and Workplace Policies. Deciding whether to disclose a workplace relationship to colleagues and supervisors is a delicate matter. Many companies have policies in place regarding office romances, and it is important to be aware of and comply with these guidelines. Transparency with human resources can mitigate potential issues and demonstrate a commitment to maintaining a professional environment.

When considering disclosure, it's crucial to understand the specific policies of your organization. Some companies require mandatory reporting of romantic relationships, especially if there is a direct reporting line involved. Being upfront about the relationship can help avoid accusations of secrecy or policy violations later on.

Approaching the disclosure conversation with your partner first ensures that you both are on the same page about how to present your relationship. When you do disclose, focus on how you plan to maintain professionalism and adhere to company policies. This can help ease any concerns from management and underscore your dedication to your role and the organization.

Navigating Breakups in the Workplace. While some workplace romances can lead to long-term partnerships, others may not withstand the test of time. Navigating a breakup within the professional environment can be particularly challenging. It is crucial to handle the situation with maturity and professionalism to minimize disruption.

Post-breakup, maintaining professionalism is key. This involves keeping personal grievances out of the workplace and avoiding any behavior that could be perceived as retaliatory or unprofessional. It's also important to communicate boundaries and establish a new normal in your interactions to prevent further discomfort.

In some cases, it might be beneficial to seek mediation or support from HR to manage the transition smoothly. HR can provide guidance on how to handle interactions and ensure that the breakup does not negatively impact your work or the broader team. Prioritizing a respectful and professional approach can help both parties move forward and maintain a positive work environment.

Leveraging Professional Support Networks. Having a robust support network within the workplace can be beneficial when managing a romantic relationship. Trusted colleagues can offer perspective and advice, helping to navigate the complexities of office romance. Additionally, professional mentors or supervisors can provide guidance on balancing personal and career aspirations.

Engaging with a mentor can offer valuable insights into how to handle a workplace relationship. Mentors can provide an objective perspective and share their own experiences, helping you navigate the challenges and opportunities that come with office romance. This guidance can be instrumental in maintaining both personal and professional growth.

Furthermore, cultivating a network of supportive colleagues can create a positive buffer. These colleagues can offer emotional support, provide feedback, and help maintain a balanced perspective. Participating in team activities and fostering strong professional relationships can ensure that your support network is robust and reliable, providing stability during times of both personal and professional change.

Conclusion: Harmonizing Love and Work. Romantic relationships at work are a reality for many individuals. The key to successfully managing such relationships lies in maintaining a balance between personal desires and professional responsibilities. By establishing clear boundaries, adhering to company policies, and approaching the relationship with transparency and respect, couples can navigate the complexities of workplace romance.

Achieving this balance requires ongoing effort and communication. Couples must continually assess and adjust their approach to ensure that their relationship remains harmonious both within and outside the workplace. This might involve regular check-ins, reassessing boundaries, and seeking external support when needed.

Ultimately, the goal is to create a harmonious environment where both love and career can thrive. With careful consideration and open communication, it is possible to enjoy the benefits of a workplace romance while preserving professional integrity and fostering a positive work culture. By navigating these challenges thoughtfully, couples can turn potential pitfalls into opportunities for growth and deeper connection.

Chapter 12
Navigating Love Across Age Differences

B*ridging the Generational Gap.* Love knows no bounds, and one of the most intriguing dynamics it explores is the interplay between partners of significantly different ages. In a society where age gaps can sometimes raise eyebrows, navigating such relationships requires finesse, understanding, and a deep appreciation for the complexities inherent in bridging generational differences. This chapter delves into the nuances of large age gap relationships, offering insights, challenges, and strategies for those embarking on this unique journey.

Understanding Perspectives. The first step in navigating a large age gap relationship is acknowledging and understanding the perspectives each partner brings to the table. Age often shapes experiences, values, and worldviews, and recognizing these differences lays the foundation for mutual respect and empathy. The younger partner may offer fresh insights, enthusiasm, and a modern outlook, while the older partner brings wisdom, stability, and a wealth of life experiences. Embracing these diverse perspectives enriches the relationship and fosters a deeper connection built on mutual learning and growth.

In large age gap relationships, embracing each other's perspectives isn't just about acknowledging differences—it's also about actively challenging preconceived notions and biases. Both partners have the opportunity to broaden their horizons and expand their worldview by engaging in open-minded discussions and exploring diverse viewpoints. Rather than viewing age as a barrier, couples can see it as a bridge that connects them to different generations, cultures, and experiences. By approaching their relationship with curiosity and a willingness to learn from each other, partners can cultivate a deep sense of mutual respect and appreciation, enriching their connection and fostering personal growth in the process.

Communication Is Key. Effective communication serves as the cornerstone of any successful relationship, but it takes on added importance in large age gap relationships. Open, honest dialogue allows partners to express their needs, concerns, and expectations, fostering understanding and trust. It's essential to create a safe space where both partners feel comfortable discussing sensitive topics such as future plans, societal perceptions, and potential challenges arising from the age gap. By actively listening to each other's viewpoints and validating their feelings, couples can navigate potential conflicts with grace and compassion.

Beyond verbal communication, nonverbal cues also play a crucial role in large age gap relationships. Partners may express their feelings through gestures, touch, or subtle nuances that reflect their emotional state. Understanding and interpreting these nonverbal signals requires sensitivity and attentiveness, fostering deeper intimacy and connection. Additionally, incorporating creative forms of communication such as writing letters, sharing art, or engaging in shared activities can enhance understanding and strengthen the bond between partners. By embracing a holistic approach to communication that encompasses both verbal and nonverbal expressions, couples can cultivate a rich and meaningful connection that transcends the limitations of words alone.

Navigating Life Stages. Ongoing communication and adaptation is vital as partners navigate changing priorities and aspirations. Couples can proactively address potential conflicts by discussing their expectations for the future and finding common ground. Establishing shared goals and milestones allows partners to align their trajectories and support each other's personal growth and development. By embracing flexibility and compromise, couples can navigate life stages with resilience and strengthen their bond in the process.

As partners in a large age gap relationship move through different life stages, it's crucial to remain adaptable and supportive of each other's evolving needs and aspirations. This may require reevaluating individual goals and priorities, as well as making compromises to ensure that both partners feel valued and respected. By approaching life stages as opportunities for mutual growth and exploration, couples can navigate transitions with grace and solidarity, forging a path forward that honors their shared journey.

Overcoming Societal Stigma. Society often imposes judgment and stigma on large age gap relationships, perpetuating stereotypes, and misconceptions. It's essential for couples to cultivate resilience and confidence in the face of external scrutiny, recognizing that love transcends age-based conventions. By focusing on the authenticity of their connection and the strength of their bond, partners can defy societal expectations and forge a relationship grounded in mutual respect and admiration. Surrounding themselves with supportive friends and family members who embrace their love story can also help mitigate the impact of external judgment.

Confronting societal stigma in large age gap relationships requires a conscious effort to redefine conventional norms and expectations. Instead of internalizing external judgments, couples can use their relationship as a platform for advocacy and change. By openly sharing their experiences and challenging misconceptions, they can spark meaningful conversations and promote greater acceptance and understanding within their communities. Embracing authenticity and resilience in the face of adversity, partners can pave the way for a more inclusive society that celebrates love in all its forms, regardless of age. Through their courage and commitment, they become trailblazers, carving out a path that encourages others to embrace diversity and reject discrimination.

Celebrating Shared Moments. Amidst the challenges and complexities, large age gap relationships offer a wealth of opportunities for shared growth and celebration. From exploring new hobbies together to embarking on adventures that span generations, couples can create cherished memories that bridge the generational divide. Embracing each other's interests, traditions, and cultural influences enriches the relationship, fostering a sense of belonging and unity. By embracing the uniqueness of their partnership and embracing the journey of love, couples can navigate the complexities of age gap relationships with grace and resilience.

Celebrating shared moments serves as a reminder of the joy and connection that defines the relationship, strengthening the bond between partners. Whether it's commemorating milestones or simply enjoying everyday moments together, finding ways to celebrate their love reaffirms its significance in their lives. Creating rituals and traditions that are meaningful to both partners fosters a sense of intimacy and belonging, deepening their connection over time. By prioritizing quality time and cultivating a spirit of gratitude, couples can nurture their relationship and create a legacy of love that transcends age.

Chapter 13
Navigating Interracial Relationships

Understanding Cultural Differences. Interracial relationships can be deeply enriching, offering partners a unique opportunity to explore and appreciate diverse cultural backgrounds. However, understanding cultural differences is essential for fostering a healthy relationship. Each partner brings their own set of traditions, values, and worldviews shaped by their cultural upbringing. This diversity can lead to enriching experiences and broader perspectives. It's important to approach these differences with curiosity and openness rather than judgment. By actively learning about each other's cultural backgrounds, couples can develop a deeper mutual respect and appreciation.

However, cultural differences can also present challenges. Misunderstandings may arise from different communication styles, family expectations, or societal norms. For example, one partner's family might have specific traditions or customs that are unfamiliar or even uncomfortable to the other. Navigating these differences requires patience, empathy, and a willingness to compromise. Open and honest communication about these issues is vital. By acknowledging and addressing cultural differences head-on, couples can find common ground and build a stronger, more resilient relationship.

Dealing with Societal Prejudices. Interracial couples often face societal prejudices that can put strain on their relationship. These prejudices can come in various forms, from subtle microaggressions to overt discrimination. Understanding and acknowledging these external pressures is crucial for maintaining a united front. It's important for partners to discuss their experiences with prejudice and to support each other in navigating these challenges. Solidarity and mutual support can help couples withstand societal judgment and reinforce their commitment to each other.

Dealing with societal prejudices also involves building a support network of friends and family who are accepting and understanding. Surrounding yourselves with positive influences can help counteract negative societal attitudes. Additionally, engaging in community activism or participating in discussions about racial issues can empower couples and contribute to a broader social change. By standing together against prejudice and fostering an inclusive environment, interracial couples can strengthen their bond and promote greater understanding and acceptance in society.

Balancing Family Expectations. Family expectations can significantly impact interracial relationships. Both partners may face pressure from their families to adhere to cultural norms and traditions, which can sometimes be at odds with their relationship. Navigating these expectations requires sensitivity and diplomacy. Open communication with family members about your relationship and its significance can help alleviate concerns and build understanding. It's crucial to approach these conversations with respect, acknowledging the importance of cultural traditions while asserting the value of your relationship.

Balancing family expectations also involves setting boundaries. Partners must prioritize their relationship and establish clear boundaries with their families to protect their bond. This might include negotiating holiday traditions, addressing disapproving family members, or finding ways to integrate both cultures into your shared life. By standing firm in your commitment to each other and addressing family concerns respectfully, you can create a harmonious balance that honors both your relationship and your cultural backgrounds.

Cultivating Mutual Respect and Understanding. Mutual respect and understanding are the cornerstones of any successful relationship, particularly in interracial partnerships. Embracing each other's cultural identities and values fosters a deep sense of respect. This involves more than just acknowledging differences; it means actively engaging with and valuing each other's cultural heritage. Celebrating cultural holidays together, learning each other's languages, and sharing stories about your backgrounds are all ways to cultivate mutual respect and understanding.

Furthermore, it's essential to address any biases or assumptions that may arise within the relationship. Partners should be willing to confront and challenge their own prejudices and work together to create an inclusive and accepting environment. This process requires ongoing effort and open dialogue. By continually striving to understand and respect each other's perspectives, interracial couples can build a strong, empathetic, and supportive relationship that transcends cultural boundaries.

Navigating Identity and Belonging. In interracial relationships, partners often navigate complex issues related to identity and belonging. Each partner's sense of self may be deeply intertwined with their cultural heritage, and finding a balance between individual and shared identities can be challenging. It's essential for both partners to support each other in exploring and expressing their cultural identities. Encouraging each other to participate in cultural practices and traditions can help maintain a sense of individuality while fostering a shared identity as a couple.

Navigating identity also involves dealing with societal perceptions and expectations. Interracial couples may feel pressured to conform to certain stereotypes or face questions about their cultural authenticity. It's crucial to resist these external pressures and focus on defining your relationship on your own terms. Open discussions about identity and belonging can strengthen your bond and help you navigate the complexities of being in an interracial relationship. By supporting each other's cultural expressions and rejecting societal labels, you can create a relationship that is true to both your identities.

Handling Misunderstandings and Conflict. Misunderstandings and conflicts are natural in any relationship, but they can be particularly pronounced in interracial relationships due to cultural differences. These conflicts often arise from miscommunications, differing values, or external pressures. Addressing misunderstandings requires patience, empathy, and effective communication. It's important to approach conflicts with a willingness to understand your partner's perspective and to express your own feelings openly and honestly.

Effective conflict resolution also involves setting aside time to discuss issues calmly and constructively. Avoiding blame and focusing on finding solutions together can help prevent conflicts from escalating. It's helpful to learn about each other's conflict resolution styles and to respect those differences. Seeking external support, such as couples counseling, can also provide valuable tools for navigating conflicts. By handling misunderstandings with care and a commitment to understanding each other, interracial couples can strengthen their relationship and overcome cultural barriers.

Building a Shared Future. Building a shared future in an interracial relationship involves blending two cultural backgrounds into a cohesive vision for your life together. This requires intentional planning and a commitment to honoring both cultures. Discussing your long-term goals and how your cultural values influence these goals can help create a unified vision. Whether it's deciding where to live, how to raise children, or how to celebrate holidays, finding ways to integrate both cultures into your shared life is key.

Building a shared future also involves addressing potential challenges proactively. Anticipating issues such as family expectations, societal prejudices, and cultural misunderstandings can help you prepare and respond effectively. By setting shared goals and working together to achieve them, you can create a strong foundation for your future.

Embracing both your individual and collective cultural identities will enrich your relationship and provide a solid basis for a lifelong partnership.

The Role of Community Support. Community support plays a crucial role in the success of interracial relationships. Finding and connecting with a community that embraces diversity can provide a valuable support network. This community can offer understanding, advice, and solidarity, helping you navigate the unique challenges of an interracial relationship. Engaging with organizations or social groups that celebrate multiculturalism can also provide opportunities to share experiences and learn from others in similar situations.

Additionally, community support can help counteract negative societal attitudes. Being part of a supportive community can reinforce your relationship and provide a sense of belonging. It's also beneficial to advocate for inclusivity and diversity within your broader community. By participating in initiatives that promote cultural understanding and acceptance, you can contribute to a more inclusive society. Building and maintaining a supportive community can significantly enhance the strength and resilience of your interracial relationship.

Celebrating Diversity in Everyday Life. Celebrating diversity in everyday life is a joyful aspect of interracial relationships. Integrating elements from both partners' cultures into your daily routines can create a rich and fulfilling shared life. This might include cooking each other's traditional dishes, participating in cultural festivals, or even incorporating different cultural practices into your home. Such practices not only enhance your bond but also enrich your lives with diverse experiences and perspectives.

Additionally, celebrating diversity involves educating any future children about both cultural backgrounds. Teaching them to appreciate and take pride in their multicultural heritage helps foster a sense of identity and belonging. It's important to create an environment where diversity is celebrated, and differences are viewed as strengths. By embracing and celebrating diversity in everyday life, interracial couples can cultivate a loving and inclusive family environment that honors both partners' cultural identities.

Chapter 14
Moving On from Heartbreak

H*ealing from a Breakup.* Healing from a breakup can be a challenging and painful process, but it is an essential step towards moving on and finding happiness again. It is important to allow yourself time to grieve and process your emotions before attempting to move on. Give yourself permission to feel sad, angry, or hurt, and don't rush the healing process. Take the time to reflect on the relationship and what you have learned from it, so you can grow and evolve from the experience.

One of the most important aspects of healing from a breakup is practicing self-care and self-love. Take time to focus on yourself and your own well-being. Engage in activities that you enjoy and that bring you happiness, whether it's spending time with friends, pursuing a hobby, or practicing mindfulness and self-care. Treat yourself with kindness and compassion and remember that you deserve to be happy and fulfilled, even after a breakup.

It can also be helpful to seek support from friends, family, or a therapist during this difficult time. Surround yourself with people who care about you and who can provide emotional support and encouragement. Talking about your feelings and experiences with others can help you process your emotions and gain perspective on the situation. A therapist can also provide valuable insights and tools for coping with the breakup and moving forward in a healthy way.

As you navigate the healing process, it is important to set boundaries with your ex-partner and take steps to distance yourself from them if necessary. This may mean unfollowing them on social media, avoiding places where you might run into them, or limiting contact with them. Creating physical and emotional distance can help you focus on yourself and your own healing journey without being constantly reminded of the past relationship.

Ultimately, remember that healing from a breakup is a journey, and it's okay to take things one day at a time. Be patient with yourself and give yourself grace as you work through your emotions and move forward. In time, you will find healing and closure, and be able to open yourself up to new opportunities and experiences in the dating scene.

Learning from Past Relationships. Learning from past relationships is a crucial aspect of personal growth and development in the dating scene. It is important to reflect on past relationships, both the successes and the failures, in order to better understand what you want and need in a partner. By examining the patterns and behaviors that have emerged in past relationships, you can gain valuable insights into your own values, desires, and boundaries.

One of the key lessons to be learned from past relationships is the importance of communication. Many relationship issues stem from a lack of communication, whether it be not expressing your needs and desires clearly or not listening to your partner's concerns. By reflecting on past relationships, you can identify areas where communication broke down and work on improving your communication skills for future relationships.

Another valuable lesson to be learned from past relationships is the importance of setting boundaries. It is essential to establish clear boundaries in a relationship in order to protect your own emotional well-being and ensure mutual respect between partners. By looking back on past relationships, you can identify instances where your boundaries were crossed or where you failed to assert your needs and use that knowledge to set healthier boundaries in the future.

Past relationships can also teach us about the importance of self-care and self-love. It is easy to lose sight of our own needs and desires when we are in a relationship, but it is crucial to prioritize self-care and ensure that we are meeting our own emotional and physical needs. By reflecting on past relationships, you can identify times when you neglected yourself in favor of your partner and work on developing a healthier balance in future relationships.

Overall, learning from past relationships is an essential part of navigating the dating scene as an adult. By examining the patterns and behaviors that have emerged in past relationships, you can gain valuable insights into your own values, desires, and boundaries. Use these lessons to improve your communication skills, set healthy boundaries, and prioritize self-care in future relationships. By learning from the past, you can create healthier, more fulfilling relationships in the future.

Embracing a Fresh Start. Embracing a fresh start in the dating scene can be both exhilarating and intimidating. It's important to approach this new chapter in your life with an open mind and a positive attitude. Leave behind any baggage from past relationships and embrace the opportunity to meet new people and create new connections. By letting go of the past, you give yourself the chance to start fresh and build something truly special.

One of the key aspects of embracing a fresh start is to be open to trying new things. This might mean stepping out of your comfort zone and exploring different ways of meeting potential partners. Whether it's trying out a new dating app, attending a singles event, or joining a new social group, being open to new experiences can lead to exciting opportunities and unexpected connections. Embrace the unknown and be willing to take risks in order to find love.

Another important element of embracing a fresh start is to focus on self-improvement and personal growth. Take this time to reflect on your own strengths and weaknesses, and work on becoming the best version of yourself. Whether it's through therapy, self-help books, or personal development courses, investing in yourself will not only make you a more attractive partner, but also help you navigate the dating scene with more confidence and self-assurance.

It's also crucial to set clear intentions and goals for what you want to achieve in your dating life. Whether you're looking for a casual fling, a long-term relationship, or something in between, being clear about your desires and boundaries will help you attract the right kind of partner. Take the time to identify what you truly want and need in a relationship, and don't settle for anything less than what you deserve.

Finally, remember to have fun and enjoy the journey. Dating can be a rollercoaster of emotions, but it's important to stay positive and keep a sense of humor throughout the process. Embrace the ups and downs, learn from your experiences, and trust that the right person will come into your life when the time is right. By embracing a fresh start with an open heart and mind, you'll be well on your way to finding the love and connection you desire.

Chapter 15
Navigating Narcissistic Relationships

Identifying Narcissistic Traits. In today's dating scene, it's important to be able to identify narcissistic traits in potential partners. Narcissism is a personality disorder characterized by a sense of entitlement, a lack of empathy, and a constant need for admiration. These traits can be toxic in a relationship and can lead to emotional abuse and manipulation. By learning to recognize these traits early on, you can protect yourself from getting involved with someone who may not have your best interests at heart.

One common trait of narcissism is a lack of empathy. Narcissists are often unable to see things from another person's perspective and may dismiss or belittle their partner's feelings. They may also be quick to blame others for their own shortcomings and may not take responsibility for their actions. If you find yourself constantly feeling misunderstood or invalidated by your partner, it may be a sign that they lack empathy and may be a narcissist.

Another key trait of narcissism is a sense of entitlement. Narcissists believe that they are special and deserving of special treatment. They may expect their partner to cater to their every need and may become angry or resentful if they don't get their way. This sense of entitlement can lead to controlling behavior and can make it difficult for their partner to assert their own needs and boundaries. If you feel like you are constantly walking on eggshells around your partner or that you can never do enough to please them, it may be a sign that they have a sense of entitlement.

Narcissists also have a constant need for admiration and validation. They may fish for compliments or constantly seek reassurance from their partner. They may also become jealous or insecure if their partner receives attention from others. This constant need for validation can be draining for their partner and can make it difficult to have a healthy, balanced relationship. If you find yourself constantly having to boost your partner's ego or if they become angry or upset when you don't give them enough attention, it may be a sign that they are a narcissist.

In conclusion, it's important to be able to identify narcissistic traits in potential partners in order to protect yourself from toxic relationships. By recognizing signs such as a lack of empathy, a sense of entitlement, and a constant need for admiration, you can avoid getting involved with someone who may not have your best interests at heart. Remember that you deserve to be in a healthy, loving relationship where your needs are respected and valued. Don't settle for anything less.

Dynamics of a Narcissistic Relationship. Narcissistic relationships can be toxic and damaging to one's mental and emotional well-being. In a narcissistic relationship, one partner, typically the narcissist, displays excessive self-importance, a lack of empathy, and a constant need for admiration. The other partner often finds themselves feeling manipulated, controlled, and emotionally drained. Understanding the dynamics of a narcissistic relationship is crucial for recognizing the signs and protecting oneself from potential harm.

One of the key characteristics of a narcissistic relationship is the imbalance of power and control. The narcissist tends to dominate the relationship, dictating the terms and expecting their partner to cater to their needs and desires. This can lead to feelings of inadequacy and worthlessness in the other partner, as they are constantly seeking validation and approval from the narcissist.

Another common dynamic in a narcissistic relationship is emotional manipulation. The narcissist may use tactics such as gaslighting, guilt-tripping, and love bombing to maintain control over their partner. They may also engage in passive-aggressive behavior or emotional blackmail to get their way. This can create a cycle of abuse and dependency, where the victim feels trapped and unable to break free from the toxic relationship.

In a narcissistic relationship, communication is often skewed, with the narcissist dominating the conversation and dismissing their partner's thoughts and feelings. The partner may feel unheard, invalidated, and constantly criticized by the narcissist. This can lead to feelings of isolation and loneliness, as the partner struggles to express themselves and connect with their narcissistic counterpart.

Ultimately, the dynamics of a narcissistic relationship are damaging and unhealthy for both parties involved. It is important for individuals to recognize the signs of narcissistic behavior in a partner and seek help if they find themselves in a toxic relationship. By setting boundaries, seeking support from friends and family, and prioritizing self-care, individuals can protect themselves from the harmful effects of a narcissistic relationship and work towards building healthier and more fulfilling connections in the future.

Strategies for Coping and Protecting Yourself. Coping with and protecting yourself from the damaging effects of a narcissistic relationship requires specific strategies. Setting clear and firm boundaries is essential to protect your emotional and physical well-being. These boundaries should be communicated assertively and maintained consistently.

Seeking support from friends, family, or a therapist can provide much-needed perspective and emotional backing. Engaging in self-care activities is crucial to nurture your mental and physical health amidst the turmoil.

Educating yourself about narcissistic personality disorder can help you recognize manipulative behaviors and respond effectively. By understanding the tactics narcissists use, you can better protect yourself and make informed decisions about the relationship.

Chapter 16
Delving Deeper: Narcissistic Dynamics

Dealing with a Narcissistic Partner. Navigating the dating scene can be challenging, especially when you find yourself in a relationship with a narcissistic partner. Narcissists are individuals who have an inflated sense of self-importance and a constant need for admiration from others. They can be charming and charismatic at first, but over time, their manipulative and self-centered behavior can take a toll on your emotional well-being. If you suspect that you are in a relationship with a narcissistic partner, it is important to take steps to protect yourself and prioritize your own mental health.

One of the key aspects of dealing with a narcissistic partner is setting boundaries. Narcissists thrive on control and manipulation, so it is important to establish clear boundaries and communicate your needs and expectations clearly. Be prepared for pushback from your partner, as narcissists often struggle to respect boundaries. Stay firm in your boundaries and do not allow yourself to be manipulated or guilt-tripped into compromising your own well-being.

It is also important to practice self-care and prioritize your own emotional health when dealing with a narcissistic partner. Narcissists can be draining and exhausting to be around, so make sure to take time for yourself and engage in activities that bring you joy and relaxation. Seek support from friends, family, or a therapist to help you navigate the challenges of being in a relationship with a narcissistic partner.

In some cases, it may be necessary to consider ending the relationship with a narcissistic partner. If your partner's behavior is consistently toxic and damaging to your mental health, it may be in your best interest to walk away. Remember that you deserve to be in a healthy and supportive relationship, and it is okay to prioritize your own well-being above staying in a toxic partnership.

Overall, dealing with a narcissistic partner requires patience, self-awareness, and a commitment to prioritizing your own mental health. By setting boundaries, practicing self-care, seeking support, and considering your options for ending the relationship, if necessary, you can navigate the challenges of being in a relationship with a narcissistic partner and protect your emotional well-being in the process. Remember that you deserve to be in a healthy and fulfilling relationship, and do not hesitate to take steps to protect yourself from the harmful effects of a narcissistic partner.

Managing Narcissistic Family Members. Handling relationships with narcissistic family members requires particular strategies due to the often-inescapable nature of familial ties. Narcissists tend to be self-absorbed and lack empathy, making it difficult to have healthy interactions with them. However, there are strategies you can use to manage these relationships and protect yourself from their negative behavior.

First and foremost, it's important to set boundaries with narcissistic family members. Clearly communicate what you will and will not tolerate in your interactions with them. This may involve limiting the amount of time you spend with them or avoiding certain topics of conversation that trigger their narcissistic tendencies. Remember, it's okay to prioritize your own well-being and mental health in these situations.

Another helpful strategy for managing narcissistic family members is to practice self-care. Make sure to take time for yourself and engage in activities that bring you joy and relaxation. By focusing on your own well-being, you can better cope with the challenges of dealing with narcissistic family members and maintain a sense of balance in your life.

It's also important to seek support from trusted friends or a therapist when dealing with narcissistic family members. Talking to someone who understands your situation can provide you with validation and guidance on how to navigate these difficult relationships. Remember, you don't have to face these challenges alone.

Lastly, it's crucial to recognize when a relationship with a narcissistic family member is toxic and may need to be reevaluated. If the negative behavior of a family member is affecting your mental health and well-being, it may be necessary to distance yourself from that person or seek professional help to establish healthier boundaries. Remember, you deserve to be in relationships that are loving and respectful, and it's okay to prioritize your own happiness and emotional well-being.

Parenting a Narcissistic Child. Parenting a narcissistic child can be a challenging and complex task for any adult. Narcissistic traits in children can manifest in various ways, such as a sense of entitlement, a lack of empathy, and a constant need for admiration and validation. It is important for parents to understand the underlying causes of narcissistic behavior in order to effectively navigate the challenges that come with parenting a child with these traits.

One of the key aspects of parenting a narcissistic child is setting clear boundaries and expectations. Children with narcissistic tendencies may struggle to understand and respect limits, so it is crucial for parents to establish firm boundaries and consistently enforce them. This can help prevent manipulative behavior and foster a sense of accountability in the child.

In addition to setting boundaries, it is important for parents to model healthy communication and empathy for their narcissistic child. By demonstrating empathy and understanding in their own interactions, parents can help their child develop these important social skills.

Encouraging open and honest communication can also help build trust and strengthen the parent-child relationship.

Another important aspect of parenting a narcissistic child is providing praise and validation in a healthy and constructive manner. While it is important to acknowledge and celebrate a child's achievements, it is equally important to teach them the value of humility and empathy. Parents can help their child develop a healthy sense of self-esteem by praising their efforts and character traits rather than just their accomplishments.

Overall, parenting a narcissistic child requires patience, understanding, and consistent guidance. By setting clear boundaries, modeling healthy communication, and providing praise and validation in a constructive manner, parents can help their child navigate their narcissistic tendencies and develop into empathetic and well-adjusted adults. It is important for parents to seek support and guidance from mental health professionals if they are struggling to cope with the challenges of parenting a narcissistic child.

Chapter 17

Conclusion: Reflections on Relationships

As we conclude this book, I hope you feel more equipped to navigate the complexities of modern relationships. Whether you've learned to craft an authentic online dating profile, recognize the signs of narcissism, or enhance your romantic life with fun and healthy recipes, you now have a toolkit to build and sustain meaningful connections.

Remember, the journey of love is as much about self-discovery as it is about finding the right partner. Embrace each experience, learn from it, and never lose sight of your worth.

Thank you for allowing me to be part of your journey, and I really hope you found this book helpful. I wish you all the happiness and fulfillment in your quest for love.

About the Author

Gracie Wells is an avid observer of human relationships and a dedicated writer. Drawing from her own life experiences and personal journey through the complexities of love, dating, and personal growth, Gracie offers a heartfelt and practical guide to navigating modern relationships. Her relatable and honest approach aims to inspire and empower readers to build healthier connections and find happiness, whether single or in a relationship. When she's not writing, Gracie enjoys cooking healthy recipes, exploring new places, practicing mindfulness, and engaging in meaningful conversations.